FORGIVENESS

FORGIVENESS

Sri Chinmoy

AUM PUBLICATIONS   NEW YORK

© 2004 Sri Chinmoy

ISBN 0-88497-049-3

Aum Publications
86-10 Parsons Blvd.
Jamaica, New York 11432

Contents

Foreword

Mistakes are an inevitable and perhaps necessary part of human life. Sometimes we do the wrong thing consciously, at other times unconsciously. No matter whether our mistakes are grave or minor, there comes a point when we need forgiveness — from God, from others whom we have hurt, even from ourselves. In this book Sri Chinmoy offers us his illumining guidance on how we may seek the divine Forgiveness that will not only transform our lives but grant us the promise and hope of a cloudless new beginning.

Overcoming Our Mistakes

O Forgiver of all my shortcomings,
    Forgive me.
A new hope is being born in my heart.
I shall cry from today on
To grow into Perfection's beauty-delight.

When we realise that we have made a serious mistake in our lives, what should we do?

When we make any mistake, consciously or unconsciously, immediately we should cry for forgiveness. If we do not ask the Supreme for forgiveness, then our own negative qualities will be intensified. With our aspiration, our prayer, our meditation, our dedication and our oneness with God's Will, we have to ask God to forgive us for all our mistakes, conscious and unconscious. We have to ask Him to illumine our unconscious mistakes so that we will become aware of them and not make them again.

If our mistakes are not forgiven, we will never have purity in our body, vital, mind and heart, and we will not be able to receive anything from God in these parts of our being. The soul is always receiving from God, because the soul is always pure. But the heart is not always pure and the body, vital and mind are all a dark jungle. If mistakes are not forgiven, then purification cannot take place in the body, vital, mind and heart. And if purity is not there, then the divine forces that we are praying for will never be able to enter permanently into our life. Only if God forgives our mistakes and we get purity in our entire consciousness will we be able to increase our receptivity and receive God's divine qualities in abundant measure.

If we pray for God's Forgiveness-Light and if our aspiration and receptivity are strong enough, definitely God's Compassion will remove the wrong forces that cause us problems and, at the same time, He will increase our soul's light to prevent them from ruining our aspiration. Aspiration is our part and Compassion and Forgiveness are God's part. No matter how many mistakes we make, God is eager to forgive us, if we give Him the chance. We also must have the enthusiasm and determination to do the right thing and not make the same mistakes over and over again, year after year.

Once we are forgiven, we will have the sweetest feeling inside our heart and inside this sweetness we will feel real purity. Then we will know that God has forgiven us. With this sweet feeling we will have tremendous eagerness and determination to please the Supreme in His own Way, and we will feel that we are only for Him. So once we feel this sweetness and eagerness to please God, we will know that God has forgiven us.

> *Two hopes are constantly singing*
> *Inside my throbbing heart:*
> *   I shall one day start loving*
> *My Lord Supreme unconditionally;*
> *   My Lord Supreme will secretly tell me*
> *That He has forgiven me everlastingly.*

How does the Supreme illumine the past?

The Supreme illumines the past by forgiveness. Real forgiveness means forgetfulness, conscious forgetfulness. Real forgiveness does not remember the past. If somebody really forgives you for something that you did, then he will not keep the memory even in his inner vision. Illumination is necessary because of darkness. Mistakes are darkness. So the Supreme illumines our mistakes through forgiveness.

> *The sunlit way to realise God*
> *Is to clearly forget*
> > *And wisely forgive*
> *One's past failures.*

If God forgives us, does that mean He will not punish us for what we have done wrong?

The Western concept of forgiveness is usually associated with guilt and retribution. You give somebody a smart slap, and afterwards you feel sad or guilty. Then the other person will curse you and say that God will punish you. Or perhaps he will threaten to strike you in retaliation. There is a feeling that if you have done something wrong, the same kind of thing will be done to you unless you are forgiven.

But there is another way to look at forgiveness. God wants us to be at a certain height so that we can receive His Affection, Love, Compassion and Blessings, but right now we are not at that level. So God is begging us: "Just raise your consciousness an iota and come up to this level.

Then I will be able to give you My Love, My Compassion and My Blessings." Our human mind may call it forgiveness, but God is not thinking about our inner and outer misdeeds. He just wants us to raise our consciousness so that we will increase our receptivity and oneness with Him. Then He will be able to give us more Compassion, more Light and more Love.

> *Only two miracles*
> *Are worth seeing:*
> *The miracle of loving*
> *And*
> *The miracle of forgiving.*

What is the essence of the forgiveness experience?

On earth, forgiveness is a sweet experience, a necessary realisation. Forgiveness is the expansion of one's reality-light and divinity-height. In Heaven, forgiveness is a supreme necessity. In God, Forgiveness is the living Breath that transcends itself each time it is used.

Is there any limit to God's Forgiveness?

As there is no limit to man's ignorance, even so, there is no limit to God's Forgiveness.

> *There is not a single shore*
> *That is untouched*
> *By God's Forgiveness-Feet.*

The Ideal of Forgiveness

My Lord Supreme,
You forgive me
And give me another chance,
    Not because
I deserve forgiveness,
    But because
You want Your entire Creation
To be absolutely perfect.

What do you mean by 'the ideal of forgiveness'?

Let me tell you a traditional Indian story by way of reply. Once there was a great king named Vishwamitra. One day he learned that there was a saint in his kingdom whom everybody adored. The name of this saint was Vashistha, and everyone gladly touched his feet. Now, although Vishwamitra was a very great king, nobody used to come and touch his feet. People were afraid of him, and they would tremble before him. But with Vashistha it was different. People gladly touched Vashistha's feet with deepest appreciation and admiration. So Vishwamitra was extremely jealous of Vashistha.

Vashistha was a very great saint. After praying to God for many, many years, Vashistha had realised God and could speak to God face to face. Vishwamitra knew that this was the reason why everybody was adoring Vashistha instead of him, so he, too, started praying to God. He prayed to God for a couple of years very seriously, often fasting, but still he did not realise God. Then he became impatient. He went to Vashistha and said, "You have realised God, but I have not been able to. I wish you to tell the world that I have also realised God, like you."

Vashistha replied, "How can I say that?"

"You *can* say it," the king insisted. "If you tell people, everybody will believe you, because you yourself have realised God. You know who God is; you speak to God. Tell everyone that I have realised God. Otherwise, I shall kill your children!"

Vashistha said, "You can kill my children, but I cannot tell a lie."

Vishwamitra was a most powerful king. One by one he had the hundred sons of Vashistha killed. The hundred sons were very well educated, kind and spiritual. They had studied the Vedas, the Upanishads and other religious and sacred books. Nevertheless, the notorious king killed them all.

Even after doing this Vishwamitra was not satisfied because Vashistha still refused to announce that he had realised God. After a few months he thought, "This time he *has* to tell the world that I have realised God, or I shall kill *him!*"

With this idea in his mind he went to Vashistha's small cottage. Before knocking at the door he stood outside quietly listening to the conversation inside. Arundhati, one of Vashistha's wives, was saying to her husband, "My lord, why do you not say that Vishwamitra has realised God? If you had said it, I would still have all my children. They were such nice, kind, devoted children. They were all jewels. But just because you would not say that he has realised God, he has killed all my children, and who knows what he will do next?"

Vashistha said, "How can you ask me to do that? I love him. He has not realised God. How can I tell people that he has realised God? I love him and that is why I cannot tell a lie." Even though Vishwamitra had killed the hundred sons of Vashistha, their father could still say that he loved him!

When Vishwamitra heard what Vashistha said, he came running in and touched Vashistha's feet, crying, "Forgive me, forgive me, forgive me, my lord. I never knew that anyone on earth could love a person who had killed his children."

Vashistha placed his hand on Vishwamitra's head and blessed him. He said, "Today you have realised God, because today you know what love is, what Truth is. God is all Forgiveness. I am forgiving you because the God in me is forgiving you. Today you have realised God."

What do we learn from this story? We learn that the ideal of forgiveness is the supreme ideal. When we pray to God, we see God's qualities: Love and Forgiveness. When we receive Love and Forgiveness from God we can behave like God towards other people. Vashistha's hundred sons were killed, yet even then he loved Vishwamitra. Then, when Vishwamitra begged for forgiveness, Vashistha gave it immediately, as well as giving him his inner light, joy and power. Like Vashistha, we always have to forgive people when they do wrong things. In this way we give them our light, our truth, our joy.

From this story we also learn the importance of associating with holy men. When we are in the company of a spiritual person, even for a second, what transformation takes place in our life! Our life is changed in the twinkling of an eye.

My Lord,
When You forgive me,
What happens You know:
I not only feel Your Heartbeats
Inside my heart,
But I also feel
That Your Compassion-Universe
Is my salvation-universe.

How to Receive God's Forgiveness

There are two ways
   To win forgiveness.
One way is to tell God,
   "My Lord,
I shall not do it again!"
The other way is to ask God,
   "My Lord,
Please show me the way
To live consciously in You
   And for You."

How can I receive God's Forgiveness?

You can receive God's Forgiveness only by reminding yourself constantly, consciously, sleeplessly and breathlessly that God is Forgiveness itself. You should not think of God as Justice or infinite Light or Peace. You should not think of any other aspect of God. You should only think of God's Forgiveness or of God the Forgiveness. You have to inundate your mind and your heart with one thought: forgiveness, forgiveness, forgiveness.

Instead of thinking of God's Justice-Light, you should just repeat: "My Lord is all Forgiveness, my Lord is all Forgiveness." While repeating, "My Lord is all Forgiveness," you must not think of all the countless mistakes that you have made. Only try to see the positive side. Think only of God's Forgiveness before you, around you and within you. If hundreds and thousands of times you can repeat most soulfully, "My Lord is all Forgiveness," then all your Himalayan blunders will be washed away. All the mistakes that you have made over the years, all the ignorant things that you have done, will be annihilated.

19

At that time, you will not only feel that you are forgiven, but you will feel that you yourself are God's Forgiveness. If someone asks you your name, you will say, "My name is my Lord's Forgiveness." If someone asks you who you are, you will say, "I am my Lord's Forgiveness." This will be your only credential.

In the ordinary life people have many credentials. They have this university degree, that degree and so on. But a spiritual seeker will have only one credential. He will say, "I am my Lord's Forgiveness," or "I am my Lord's Compassion," or "I am my Lord's Love." If somebody asks you what your credentials are, immediately you will say, "My Lord's Compassion is my only credential," or "My Lord's Forgiveness is my only credential."

This is not just false humility, for in the inmost recesses of your heart you will feel that your only credential is God's Compassion or God's Forgiveness. This is what all seekers must feel.

You forgive me;
        Therefore, I am still alive.
You love me;
        Therefore, I am still alive.
You have caught my hand;
        Therefore, I am still alive.
I am Your Compassion-Flute;
        Therefore, I am still alive.

How do you deal with guilt if you have been brought up with the feeling that God will punish you if you do something wrong?

In the Western world, unfortunately, the feeling of guilt is widespread. It comes from ignorance. First we do something wrong out of ignorance and then we have a guilty conscience. Instead, immediately we must think, "If I have the power to do something wrong, then God has the power to forgive me." We must not feel that no power in the universe can obliterate our wrong deeds. We have done something wrong, granted, but God is infinitely stronger than we are, and He is all

21

Compassion. Whenever we meditate, we should feel that God is all Love. He is not going to punish us. With His infinite Compassion He is going to transform us. But if we cherish a feeling of guilt, God will not be able to come to our rescue.

> *There is no crime*
> *That God cannot forgive,*
> *But we have to spend*
> *Many sleepless nights and days*
> *At His Forgiveness-Feet.*

If I do something wrong and ask the Supreme to forgive me, how do I know whether He has forgiven me?

There are two ways you can know. If you never do that kind of thing again, rest assured that the Supreme has forgiven you, for He has given you the capacity not to do it again. On the practical level, if you have done something wrong and you do not want to do it again, that means that a higher Power has come from the Supreme to protect you and give you the capacity not to do the thing again. It is because the Supreme has forgiven you that you are not making that mistake any more.

Another way is to ask your spiritual Master if the Supreme has forgiven you. The Master will be able to tell you. He will be very frank. Or you can go deep within for half an hour or an hour, and then you will be able to tell. Each time a thought comes, do not allow it to enter into your mind. Feel that a fly has come to sit on you, and chase it away. When another thought comes, chase it away, too. After a while, the thought-fly will feel that it is beneath its dignity to bother you, and then the thought-process will stop. When you see that no thought is coming, just ask the question. If the answer is "yes," then it means that God has forgiven you.

> *A sea of peace rules my heart*
> *Only after God's Forgiveness*
> *Has ruled my mind.*

If a person feels that God is all-forgiving, won't that make it easier for the person to do the wrong thing?

You feel that if one goes to the Father after doing something wrong and sees that he is forgiven, then he will be tempted to keep doing wrong things, with the feeling that he will always be forgiven. Even the human father, not to speak of the divine Father, the Almighty Father, will tell the child, "Look, you have done something wrong; you have struck another child. Just because I love you, I have forgiven you, but you cannot go on doing wrong things." If the child for a second time strikes another child and then comes back to the father, the father will protect the child. Afterwards, secretly and silently the father will say, "This is the second time that I am telling you the difference between good and bad." Each time the father will forgive, but at the same time, he will try to convince the child that he is doing something wrong.

In the case of God the divine Father, it is different. When the aspirant makes a mistake and runs towards the divine Father, the divine Father will forgive and protect the aspirant, without doubt. Then immediately the Father will try to enter into the heart of the aspirant with Light. The human father will scold secretly, but the divine Father will not scold; He knows that scolding is of no use. He tries to see what is wrong in the aspirant. He sees that darkness is there, ignorance is there, and says, "If I enter into the aspirant with Light, the Light will chase away the darkness. Then the Light will illumine the ignorance and transform it into knowledge and wisdom. This wisdom will make the aspirant feel that he should remain peaceful, calm, quiet, and not run into conflict with anybody." The divine Father accomplishes this by pouring Light into the aspirant.

The human father will protect openly and then scold secretly, but the divine Father will use pure Light to illumine our darkness and chase away the wrong forces in us. In both cases, the mistake will be overcome. The human father will conquer it through strict discipline, and the divine Father will conquer it through Light. But that does not mean that we will continue committing mistakes and then go to our Father for forgiveness.

Lord Supreme, You have forgiven me.
You have forgiven the teeming lapses
   Of Your servant.
I am always intoxicated by beauty's love,
But You have made me immaculate.
My gratitude-heart I have offered to You
And You have offered me Your Promise-Light.
You have accepted the animal in me,
The human in me, the divine in me
   As Your very own.

How is it possible to have a good meditation in the morning when we have gone to bed in a very bad consciousness?

Our good meditation does not depend on what we did yesterday. The Supreme forgives us every night while we are sleeping. If not, we would not struggle to get up the next morning. We would just say, "It is useless to try to meditate today when I was so undivine yesterday. Let me just sleep." His Forgiveness gives us the capacity to meditate well the following day. His Forgiveness is unconditional.

God empties our inner receptivity-vessel at night so that we can fill ourselves with His divine Light in the morning. That is the spiritual reason for sleep, and that is why we should always meditate early in the morning before we begin our daily activities. Once we have the spiritual capacity to empty our inner vessel ourselves, and invoke the Light of the Supreme, then we will be able to transcend sleep.

> *Although you yourself*
> *Have written your life-story,*
> *You are now dying to forget*
> > *Quite a few chapters.*
> *Lo, God's Forgiveness-Magic-Wand*
> > *Is poised right over your head.*

Are you there, God?
Would You mind
  Coming over to me
With Your Compassion-Eye
  And Your Forgiveness-Heart?

Forgiving Ourselves
and the World

To err is human,
But be careful,
Do not overdo it.

If to forgive is divine,
Then rest assured,
You can never overdo it.

How can we remember to forgive the world for its defects and to forgive ourselves for our own defects?

Forgiveness is a powerful divine force. To forgive others is a difficult task. To forget others' imperfections is more difficult. Not to notice anything wrong in others is most difficult. But when we think of God, it will become easy for us to forgive others. When we pray to God, it will become easy to forget others' shortcomings, limitations and imperfections. When we meditate on God, it will become easy for us not to notice anything wrong in others.

On rare occasions we see imperfection in ourselves, but we always see imperfections in others. Now, when we discover that we are imperfect or have done something wrong, what do we do? We forgive ourselves immediately, or we ignore the fact that we have done something wrong, or we decide to turn over a new leaf and never do it again.

If others do something wrong, if we do not forgive them, if we harbour undivine thoughts against them or want to punish them, we will never find true satisfaction. In order to satisfy ourselves, our reality, we must forgive others, too. Forgiveness is illumination. We have to feel that by forgiving others we are illumining ourselves, our own enlarged, expanded Self.

If we do not forgive, what happens? We place a heavy load on our shoulders. If I have done something wrong and I do not try to forgive myself or illumine myself, I will harbour the idea that I have made a mistake. And each time I think of my wrong action I will only add to my heavy load of guilt. Similarly, if others have done me an act of injustice, the more I think of this, the heavier becomes my load of anger and resentment. Now, I have to run towards my goal. If I place something heavy on my shoulders, how am I going to run? I will see that others are all running very fast, while I can hardly walk.

It is always advisable to forgive others and to forgive oneself. Again, we have to know who is forgiving whom. I, as an individual, have no right to forgive others or even to forgive myself. It is the Divine within me that is inspiring me to raise my consciousness to Light, to higher Light, to highest

Light. An act of forgiveness means a movement to a higher reality. And when we reach the highest Reality, we become one with the omnipresent Reality.

We are all integral parts of a living organism. If I have only two arms, I am incomplete. I need two legs, too. So I have to accept others as my very own. First I accept them, and then I transform them. And whom am I transforming, if not my own expanding reality?

> *Forgive,*
>   *You will have happiness.*
> *Forget,*
>   *You will have satisfaction.*
> *Forgive and forget,*
>   *You will have everlasting peace*
> *Within and without.*

I find it especially hard to forgive myself when I do something wrong because I feel that it is a set-back in my spiritual life.

Whenever you do something wrong, God will forgive you and your spiritual Master will forgive you, but there is someone who may not forgive you and that is your soul. The soul does not forgive so easily because the soul knows that due to this particular mistake, this deliberate mistake, it will have to reincarnate on earth for many more years. Each time you make a conscious mistake, your soul knows that it is like going a hundred steps backwards. So naturally you are delaying your journey instead of expediting it.

The soul is the eldest brother in the inner family, and it has promised the Supreme Father that the younger members will be taken care of. The soul is fully responsible for your life. When the soul sees that the younger members are not listening and the soul has to account for it, at that time the soul feels miserable.

The soul cannot forgive the younger members of the family—the body, vital, mind and heart—

when they do not listen to it, because
a task to accomplish for God. If the sou̲ ̲̲̲ows its
family to be uncooperative, then the soul will not
be able to fulfil God's Vision on earth. God, out of
His infinite Bounty, will forgive the body, vital
and mind because He deals with Eternity. But the
soul knows that each human incarnation is the
golden opportunity to manifest God. Each second
that the body, vital and mind do not listen to it is a
missed opportunity. When an opportunity is missed,
the soul feels that God-manifestation is a far cry.

> *Again and again*
> *You are making the same mistake*
> *And asking others to forgive you.*
> *But what right do you have*
> *To expect and demand their forgiveness*
> *As long as you continue*
> *Making the same mistake?*

What main qualities do I need to achieve happiness?

The two main qualities you need are gratitude and
forgiveness. You have to feel grateful to the

Supreme that you are leading a spiritual life. And you have to have forgiveness-power for others, no matter how much they criticise you or speak ill of you. From these two divine realities you will get real happiness, and in your happiness is your progress.

Judge nothing;
You will be happy.
My own personal experience
I am sharing with you.

Forgive everything;
You will be happier.
My own personal realisation
I am sharing with you.

Love everything;
You will be happiest.
God's own personal Secret
I am sharing with you.

Please tell me what to do when I feel rejected by others.

When you feel rejected by others, the human in you may be sad, frustrated or furious. But the divine within you will immediately pray to the Supreme for forgiveness for them. The only way they will get illumination is if the Supreme forgives them.

Suppose I have rejected you. The human in you may immediately become furious and try to take revenge, or it may withdraw from me. You will want to have nothing to do with me because I have rejected you or insulted you. But at that time the divine in you will try to come forward with compassion, because it knows that I have made a serious mistake in rejecting you. If you also reject me, then in what way are you superior to me? What I have done is wrong. It is very bad, true, but if you do not want to do the same wrong thing, then you have to forgive me and you have to ask God to forgive me as well.

The Saviour Christ prayed, "Father, forgive them, for they know not what they do." Similarly, you should pray to God on behalf of the one who has rejected you, who is the real culprit at that time. This is the first thing required. Secondly, you should pray to God for his illumination, so that he does not reject you or anyone else in the future. If he is really forgiven and illumined by the Supreme, then he will not reject you again.

If you reject someone who has rejected you, then both of you will be swimming in the sea of ignorance. He has done something wrong, and you are doing the same thing. Paying him back in his own coin does not serve any purpose. What you want, after all, is the illumination of humanity.

> *True, you are on your own,*
> *But you are not alone.*
> *God's Compassion-Eye*
> *And Forgiveness-Heart*
> *Can never disown you,*
> *Never!*

How can I protect myself spiritually from being too sensitive and having my feelings hurt too easily?

When somebody says something to you and you are hurt, you have to know that your forgiveness-power is infinitely more powerful than the hurt you have received. If someone has insulted you and you also insult the person, it means that you are fighting back on the same level. But your forgiveness-power is the most powerful force in God's Creation. If you use it, those people will not be able to hurt you.

> *Learn the art of forgiving*
> *And apply it to yourself first.*
> *Then it becomes easy*
> *To forgive others.*

How can we become more tolerant and understanding?

First think of how many millions of things you have done wrong in this lifetime. You will be able to count at least ten undivine things. Out of millions of things you have done wrong, you will be sincere enough to admit at least ten things. Then ask yourself if anybody has forgiven you. Naturally God has forgiven you. If He had not forgiven you, by this time you would have been in the other world. But when somebody else does something wrong, you become angry and want to punish that person. Try to count how many things that person has done wrong to you. He may have done many, many things wrong in his life, but perhaps he has done only two things wrong to you; whereas you are the culprit for at least ten individual items, and the Supreme has forgiven you.

Yesterday I did something wrong, and God forgave me. How is it that today I cannot identify myself with someone else and feel that the very thing that he has done, I could have done? What he has done wrong today, I can easily do tomorrow. I should be grateful to God that I did not do it today, and remember that tomorrow there is every possibility that I will do that very same thing,

We should sympathise with the person who has done something wrong or, on the strength of our oneness, we should tolerate it. Tolerance is not an act of weakness. Far from it! Tolerance is the acceptance of reality at a different level of consciousness. Mother Earth, the trees, the oceans and the mountains—do they not tolerate us? We abuse them in millions of ways. Yet they forgive us and nourish us continually. We are able to use them for our own purposes.

Divine tolerance is based on oneness. In the case of divine tolerance, when somebody does something wrong to me, I do not actually forgive that person. What happens is that my inner divinity becomes totally one with the person who has made a mistake and is creating a disturbance in my life. So divine tolerance is even deeper than forgiveness. It is nothing but the conscious feeling or awareness of our oneness with others. I do not tolerate you because I feel that I am superior or because I feel that I have capacity while you have none. It is all oneness.

> *When I choose*
> *To forgive the world,*
> *My divinity-sun immediately increases*
> *Its unhorizoned power.*

> *When I choose*
> *To live the life of oneness-love,*
> *My humility-moon immediately increases*
> *Its beauty's light and purity's height.*

If you want to transform
Your life radically,
Then immediately give up
Your false sense of teeming guilt.

Injustice and Forgiveness

It pains my Lord so severely
When I pray to Him to come to me
 With His Compassion-Heart,
And to go
To the rest of the world's citizens
 With His Justice-Mind.

How can we forgive injustice?

When we think of injustice in human terms, we have to go to the very depths of our realisation. When we came into the world, we made a solemn promise to God that we would realise God, manifest God and fulfil God here on earth. This was our most sincere, most soulful promise to God. When we made that promise, we were in the soul's world. We did not have the physical body; our real existence was the soul. At that time the soul said, "I am descending into the world only to please You, to fulfil You, to manifest You unconditionally."

These people whom you feel are very unjust have done something undivine, true. But look at your own promise. You expect from these people perfection; you feel they have to do everything in a perfect way. But perfection comes only when we fulfil our promise. Our first and foremost promise was to God, to please Him and fulfil Him on earth. We have not fulfilled our promise; yet we expect others to fulfil their promise. As spiritual people, we should always see what we have done wrong. Millions of things we have done wrong. If we do millions of things wrong, then naturally

God is forgiving us. Otherwise, we would not be able to exist on earth. If He is ready to forgive us in spite of our countless defects and mistakes, how is it that we cannot forgive someone else?

A spiritual seeker immediately claims himself to be a chosen child of God. An unaspiring person, a person who is wallowing in the pleasures of ignorance, would never dare to claim this. He does not dare to claim God as his very own. But you do dare to claim that you are God's chosen child, just because you have received an iota of God's good qualities. God is good, God is divine, God is perfect—all these divine qualities you have received to some extent. So if one of God's qualities is forgiveness and, if God forgives you twenty-four hours a day, can you not forgive another person for one second? If our Source has the capacity to do something in infinite measure, naturally we also should have the capacity to forgive or illumine others who have done something wrong, according to our own standard.

My life is forgiven by God.
Therefore, my heart feels obliged
To forgive the world around me.

I would like to tell a story about injustice that is at once amusing and illumining.

A young man of twenty-eight opened a stationery shop to make better use of his idle hours. Monetary gain was, for him, secondary. He was a great aspirant and had a famous spiritual Master as his Guru.

One day, while he was in his shop chanting his favourite verses from the Upanishads, a stocky man of about forty-five walked in. His complexion was unusually ugly and—although his name was Hanuman, after the monkey-Chief of the Ramayana—his face resembled that of a tiger. He was the conductor of the local opera company and everyone hated him for his rude manner. He shouted aggressively at the owner of the shop, "Stop singing! Stop singing, you so-called pious man!"

The aspirant became silent.

"When are you going to return my money?" continued the intruder. "How many times have I asked you to give me my money back? Is it not a pity that I have to remind you so many times about my money?"

The young man remained silent.

"I hear that every year you go out on a pilgrimage. You visit temples and spiritual places to acquire virtue. How do you reconcile your outer life with your so-called spiritual life? Your outer life is full of deception!"

The shopkeeper said nothing.

"It is a pity that God tolerates a scoundrel like you," the man continued his tirade. "In His Name you do so many evil things—deception being the least of them! We who admittedly have very little to do with God care much about maintaining a moral life, a life of integrity. But you who are constantly uttering the Name of God, you who are intoxicated with words like 'divinity', 'love', and 'mercy' are far more apt to deceive people—not just once, but day in, day out!"

The attack mounted, the customer's voice becoming louder and more pugnacious. "It is beneath my dignity, in fact, even to speak to you. I knew your father, who was also a man of unscrupulous character. No wonder—like father, like son!"

It happened that the youngest brother of the

shopkeeper, an athlete twelve years of age, was at the back of the store, busily pumping air into his football. Until now, this boy had tolerated the insults of the customer, but upon hearing his deceased father's name besmirched, he flew into a rage and came running to the front of the store. He was about to lunge at the customer and punch him in the nose, but the forgiving eyes of his elder brother, looking at the man with deep compassion, abruptly stopped the boy.

The customer, in a tone that was now quick and trembling, demanded again, "Why do you not give me my money back? I just want to have my money back and that is all. My time is as precious as yours."

The boy, puzzled, spoke out on behalf of his elder brother. "What money? When did you give it? How much? And to whom did you give it?"

With a defensive smile, the customer said, "Young man, I shall answer all your questions, one by one. How much money? Two hundred rupees. When was it given? Two years ago. To whom was it given?" There was a momentary pause as the customer struck his own chest with his fist. "To this rascal!" he cried, indicating himself.

The next instant he flung himself at the feet of the shopkeeper. "Forgive me! Forgive me!" he cried, his eyes flooding with tears. "I have never seen, and perhaps will never see again a man like you who is forgiveness incarnate. It is I who am the culprit. I have been trying in every way to trick you, to arouse anger in you, to make your blood boil, but I must confess that I have failed."

"I have also failed," he continued, "to keep my promise to you, my promise of two years ago. When you loaned me money, I said I would return it in two months' time. Never have you reminded me of that loan, never!" The customer continued in his bitter remorse, "I have had many experiences of borrowing money, and all my creditors became loan sharks. It is here for the first time that I have seen the magnanimity of forgiveness.

"You have forgiven my ignorance. You have awakened my soul. You have illumined my life."

> *The ghost*
> *Of my deplorable misdeeds*
>   *Disappeared*
> *The moment my mind devotedly sat*
>   *At God's Forgiveness-Feet.*

Divine Justice is nothing short of divine Forgiveness. Human justice says that if somebody has stolen something, he has to be punished. Human justice tells us that this is the right thing, and it gets tremendous pleasure by punishing the person. But when the divine Justice operates, even if it takes an outer form, inside this Justice there is tremendous compassion. While the inner judge is telling the world that so-and-so is the culprit, he is illumining the person's mind so that he does not enter into ignorance again. So when divine Justice is offered, there is an inner compassion and an inner illumination inside it. They work together so the seeker does not fall again and again into the sea of ignorance.

When human justice operates, the culprit knows that nobody has instigated him. He knows he has been responsible all the time. But divine Justice helps the culprit to realise that it is not he who has committed the wrong act, but something else which we call ignorance which has operated in and through him. When divine Justice operates, the person feels miserable that he has allowed some wrong forces to enter into him and act in and through him. He feels he was a fool to allow somebody or something else to operate in and through him. He realises he should act only according to his own inner will, according to his soul's divine guidance.

In the human court we see all kinds of crime but in the Court of Divine Justice we notice only one crime every day, and that is human ungratefulness. Here the punishment is forgiveness. Constantly the game is being played between God's Forgiveness and man's ungratefulness. In the human way, human beings are justifying their cause by saying, "We are unconscious. Hence, we commit crimes. We are not yet illumined. Hence, we are ungrateful." In the divine way, God is justifying His cause: He is Love. Hence, He is all-Loving. He is Compassion. Hence, He is all-Forgiving.

Compassion and Forgiveness

My dear Lord,
How can I live
Without Your Life's Compassion-Eye?

My sweet Lord,
How can I breathe
Without Your Heart's Forgiveness-Sky?

What comes first, God's Forgiveness or God's Compassion?

If God does not forgive me for the undivine things that I have done over the years, then how can I walk along the spiritual path, the sunlit path? Only if God forgives me can I enter wholeheartedly into the spiritual life. So, to start with, I need God's Forgiveness.

Then, when I feel that God, out of His infinite Bounty, has forgiven me, at that time I can think of another aspect of God, and that is God's Compassion. God has forgiven me; now I need His Compassion. I need His Compassion because I am weak, I am ignorant and I am in every way a failure. I fervently desire to do something, but I do not have the capacity to do what I want to do or to grow into what I want to become. Therefore, I desperately need God's Compassion. Without God's Compassion, I will not be able to achieve anything, and I will not be able to become anything.

> *I cling to God's*
> *Forgiveness-Feet.*
> *His Compassion-Eye*
> *All-where I meet.*

What is the connection between compassion and forgiveness?

Compassion and forgiveness are two different things. Let us say a mischievous little boy strikes you unnecessarily hard. You can strike him much harder, but you do not. Why? Because you have forgiven him. Then you see another little boy, all alone. He is unable to cross the street by himself because he is afraid. At that time you go and help him. You wait for the light and you take him across the street. This is your compassion.

So this is how you can separate compassion from forgiveness. Somebody needs your help, and you have the strength, you have the capacity, to be of service to him. At that time you are showing your compassion. Somebody else is unable to conquer their wrong forces. There you are offering your forgiveness. These two divine qualities are of supreme necessity every day in our life. The Supreme has Compassion and Forgiveness in infinite measure. With His Compassion-Eye, He follows us everywhere. Again, with His Forgiveness-Heart, He forgives all our wrong thoughts and actions.

We not only have to forgive others, but we also have to forgive ourselves. If we do not forgive ourselves all the time, we shall be displeased with ourselves. We have to forgive ourselves with the proper understanding that we shall not make the same mistake again; we shall go forward. Let us say that a few months ago I did something really wrong. Now I shall pray to God for forgiveness, forgiveness, forgiveness. God has already forgiven me because of my sincere prayers, but I am not forgiving myself because I have no idea that God has forgiven me. So I am the culprit. God has already forgiven me, but I have not forgiven myself. If we do not forgive ourselves, then we are unable to go forward. We are only looking backward. We have to forgive our past; otherwise we cannot enter into the future.

> *The more I try*
> *To hide my weaknesses*
> *From God,*
> *The sooner God's*
> *Compassion-Forgiveness-Radar*
> *Finds me.*

Can a human being embody both compassion and forgiveness?

As the true oneness-friend of mankind, Jesus Christ flooded the earth-consciousness with compassion and forgiveness. His immortal prayer, "Father, forgive them, for they know not what they do," will forever draw down God's Compassion and Forgiveness from Above for the inwardly hungry and thirsty truth-seekers and God-lovers. Indeed, Jesus' self-offering life and earth-illumining message will shine bright, brighter, brightest in the aspiring heart and God-loving life of humanity throughout Eternity.

My Lord, my Lord, my Lord,
Forgive me, forgive me, forgive me.
I took You for granted;
    Therefore, I failed.
But now I shall make another attempt.
This time I shall sleeplessly pray to You
So that You can inundate my prayer-life
    With Your infinite Compassion.

If a person is genuinely good, will his compassion flow through his forgiveness?

Yes. I am reminded of a story about one of the Moghul Emperors. There was nothing that the great Emperor Babar would hesitate to do for his subjects. He used to regard his subjects as his own children. From time to time, Babar used to go out of the palace grounds and walk along the streets and through the markets to mix with his subjects and see for himself the conditions in which they were living. Often, if he saw someone who was poverty-stricken, he would help that person with a little money or food. People did not recognise their Emperor during these wanderings because he would dress very simply. Also, he wore a kind of turban over his crown to disguise it.

Now it happened that there was a young man who cherished tremendous jealousy towards Babar because everybody appreciated, admired and adored the Emperor. Babar's subjects always extolled him to the skies for his bravery, kindness, nobility and other divine qualities. For this reason, the young man had been harbouring a desire to kill Babar. He had heard that from time to time the Emperor walked in the city all alone. So this young man always carried a sword, hoping that someday he would meet the Emperor when he did not have his bodyguards with him and then have the opportunity to kill the Emperor.

Usually, when Babar went out, his guards would secretly follow him to protect him. Although Babar did not want anyone to go with him, his guards were afraid for his safety. Babar was the ruler of the whole empire, but in this respect his own bodyguards would not listen to him.

One particular afternoon, Babar managed to walk out of the palace alone, without his guards.

As usual, he went incognito. As he was walking along observing the daily activities of his subjects, he saw a mad elephant coming down the street. The elephant was trampling everything in sight. Pandemonium broke out. People were shouting and trying to escape from the elephant's path and everybody was panicking. But there was one little, helpless child who could not run fast enough to get out of the elephant's way. Everybody was frightened to death, but nobody dared to try to save the child. Just as the elephant was about to trample the little child, the Emperor ran over at top speed and snatched the child out of the way. Babar saved the child, but as he was running away with the child in his arms, his turban fell to the ground.

When the mad elephant had passed by, some men ran to pick up the turban of the brave hero. Immediately they saw the Emperor's crown inside the turban. The young man who had wanted to kill Babar was one of those who witnessed the whole scene. Although he himself had known that the child's life was in grave danger, he had not been brave enough to try to save him. He had run away, just like everybody else. When he realised what had happened, he fell at Babar's feet and said, "O Emperor, forgive me."

Babar asked him, "What have you done?"

The man replied, "I have been cherishing the desire to kill you for many years because I was terribly jealous of the admiration you receive. Now I see that you truly deserve it. As Emperor, you are far more precious to the kingdom than any of us, but you were ready to give up your own life to save an ordinary human being. What I have learned from you is that it is infinitely better to give life than to take life. This is what you have taught me. Now, instead of taking life, I am giving you mine. Please take my life."

Then he offered Babar the selfsame sword with which he had planned to kill him.

Babar took the sword and said, "I taught you how to give life. Now I am going to take your life, but not in the way that you think. Come with me. From now on, you will be one of my bodyguards. I can see that your sincerity is truly remarkable and I am sure that you will be a faithful guard."

So Babar took the man's life, only to make it

into a useful and fruitful one. Instead of killing him, instead of punishing him, Babar made the man one of his personal bodyguards.

> *God's Forgiveness finds me*
> *No matter where I am.*
> *God's Compassion takes me*
> *Where I ought to go.*

I shall wait until You call.
But please call me soon.
    I have so much to say to You.
    I have so much to learn from You.
    I have so much to unlearn
By the touch of Your Forgiveness-Feet.

Prayers for Forgiveness

O my life's Lord Supreme,
Sleeplessly I invoke You
To forgive me today.
O Great One, O world's Reality-Salvation,
May I be fully awakened
In purity's auspicious dawn.

Forgive me, my Lord Supreme,
    Forgive me!
I have drunk doubt-poison
    Profusely and happily.
Now I want to change my drink.
I want to drink faith-nectar
    Immeasurably and spontaneously.
Will You not give me another chance, my Lord,
    Will You not?

Forgive me, my Lord Supreme,
    Forgive me!
I have made friends
With tenebrous ignorance-night
    Consciously and deliberately.
Now I want to change my friend.
I want to accept wisdom-light
As my new friend
    Immediately and permanently.
Will You not give me another chance, my Lord,
    Will You not?

Forgive me, my Lord Supreme,
> *Forgive me!*
I have not loved You
> *Sleeplessly and unconditionally.*
Will You not give me another chance, my Lord,
> *Will You not?*

Forgive me, my Lord Supreme,
> *Forgive me!*
I have not served You
> *Soulfully and unreservedly*
Inside the hearts of the pilgrim-seekers
Walking along Eternity's Road.
Will You not give me another chance, my Lord,
> *Will You not?*

My Lord Beloved Supreme, I do not think of
You. Yet You forgive me.

My Lord Beloved Supreme, I do not pray to
You. Yet You forgive me.

My Lord Beloved Supreme, I do not meditate
on You. Yet You forgive me.

My Lord Beloved Supreme, I do not serve
You. Yet You forgive me.

My Lord Beloved Supreme, I do not love
You. Yet You forgive me.

My Lord Beloved Supreme, I do everything
wrong and I say everything wrong. Yet You forgive me at every moment. Why, why, my Lord
Beloved Supreme?

"My child, I am the eternal Dreamer and you
are My Eternity's Dream. In My Existence-
Consciousness-Reality I am dreaming in and
through you at every moment. You want satisfaction. By not thinking of Me, by not praying to
Me, by not meditating on Me, by not serving Me,
by not loving Me, you will never have satisfaction.
You can have satisfaction only by loving Me and
claiming Me as your own, very own.

"In My case, too, I cannot get satisfaction, full satisfaction, unless I can make you a perfect seeker and a perfect human being. Throughout Eternity I have been longing for humanity's perfection. This perfection needs My infinite Compassion and My birthless and deathless Forgiveness. If necessary, I shall wait throughout Eternity to make each creation of Mine perfectly perfect, for this is My Eternity's Dream.

"I forgive you because I know there shall come a time when you will become a choice instrument of Mine. Not only that, you will become My representative here on earth. In you and through you I shall bless the world with a special Message: the Message of universal oneness.

"My child, do not be sad that you do not think of Me, that you do not pray to Me, that you do not meditate on Me, that you do not serve Me and that you do not even love Me. Do not be doomed to disappointment. There shall come a time when you will be awakened, fully awakened. My unconditional Compassion will awaken your entire being, your earthly life. Then you will think of Me sleeplessly, pray to Me breathlessly, meditate on

Me soulfully, serve Me self-givingly and love Me unconditionally. That golden Hour is fast approaching. I am all Love, and you, My child, must be fully prepared to receive Me with all your heart's love and love, gratitude and gratitude."

About Sri Chinmoy

Sri Chinmoy is a fully realised spiritual Master dedicated to inspiring and serving those seeking a deeper meaning in life. Through his teaching of meditation, his music, art and writings, his athletics and his own life of dedicated service to humanity, he tries to offer ways of finding inner peace and fulfilment.

Born in Bengal in 1931, Sri Chinmoy entered an ashram (spiritual community) at the age of 12. His life of intense spiritual practice included meditating for up to 14 hours a day, together with writing poetry, essays and devotional songs, doing selfless service and practising athletics. While still in his early teens, he had many profound inner experiences and attained spiritual realisation. He remained in the ashram for 20 years, deepening and expanding his realisation, and in 1964 came to

New York to share his inner wealth with sincere seekers.

Today, Sri Chinmoy serves as a spiritual guide to students in centres around the world. He advocates "the path of the heart" as the simplest way to make rapid spiritual progress. By meditating on the spiritual heart, he teaches, the seeker can discover his own inner treasures of peace, joy, light and love. The role of a spiritual Master, according to Sri Chinmoy, is to instruct his students in the inner life and to elevate their consciousness so that these inner riches can illumine their lives. He asks his students to meditate regularly and to nurture the inner qualities he helps them bring to the fore.

Sri Chinmoy teaches that love is the most direct way for a seeker to approach the Supreme. When a child feels love for his father, it does not matter how great the father is in the world's eye; through his love the child feels only his oneness with his father and his father's possessions. This same approach, applied to the Supreme, permits the seeker to feel that the Supreme and His own Eternity, Infinity and Immortality are the seeker's own.

This philosophy of love, Sri Chinmoy feels,

expresses the deepest bond between man and God, who are aspects of the same unified consciousness. In the life-game, man fulfils himself in the Supreme by realising that God is his own highest Self. The Supreme reveals Himself through man, who serves as His instrument for world-transformation and perfection.

Sri Chinmoy does not charge a fee for his spiritual guidance, nor does he charge for his frequent concerts or public meditations. His only fee, he says, is the seeker's sincere inner cry. He takes a personal interest in each of his students, and when he accepts a student, he takes full responsibility for that individual's inner progress. In New York, Sri Chinmoy meditates in person with his students several times a week and offers regular meditation sessions for the general public. Students living outside New York see Sri Chinmoy during worldwide gatherings that take place three times a year, during visits to New York or during the Master's frequent trips to their cities. They find that the inner bond between Master and student transcends physical separation. Sri Chinmoy accepts students at all levels of spiritual development, from beginners to advanced seekers, and lovingly guides them inwardly and outwardly according to their individual needs.

Sri Chinmoy personally leads an active life, demonstrating most vividly that spirituality is not an escape from the world, but a means of transforming it. He has written over a thousand books, which include plays, poems, stories, essays, commentaries and answers to questions on spirituality. He has painted thousands of mystical paintings, and his drawings of "soul-birds" number in the millions. He has also composed thousands of devotional songs. Performing his own musical compositions on a wide variety of instruments, he has offered hundreds of "Concerts of Prayerful Music" in cities around the world.

A naturally gifted athlete and a firm believer in the spiritual benefits of physical fitness, Sri Chinmoy encourages his students to participate in sports. Under his inspirational guidance, the international Sri Chinmoy Marathon Team organises hundreds of road races, including the longest certified race in the world (3,100 miles). In the field of weightlifting Sri Chinmoy has also achieved phenomenal feats of strength, demonstrating that inner peace gained through meditation can be a tangible source of outer strength.

For more information about Sri Chinmoy, to learn how to become his student, or to attend free meditation classes at a Sri Chinmoy Centre near you, please contact:

Aum Publications
86-10 Parsons Blvd.
Jamaica, NY 11432

or visit:

www.srichinmoy.org

Other Books by Sri Chinmoy

Grace
In the same format as *Forgiveness,* Sri Chinmoy describes the constant flow of Grace from Above and explains how we can become more receptive to it. $5.00

Meditation: Man-Perfection in God-Satisfaction
Presented with the simplicity and clarity that have become the hallmark of Sri Chinmoy's writings, this book is easily one of the most comprehensive guides to meditation available. $9.95

Beyond Within: A Philosophy for the Inner Life
Sri Chinmoy offers profound insight into humanity's relationship with God, and sound advice on how to integrate the highest spiritual aspirations into daily life. $13.95

My Life's Soul-Journey: Daily Meditations for Ever-Increasing Spiritual Fulfilment
In this volume of daily meditations, each day's offering resonates with the innate goodness of

humanity and encourages the reader to bring this goodness to the fore. $13.95

Death and Reincarnation
This deeply moving book has brought consolation and understanding to countless people faced with the loss of a loved one or fear of their own mortality. Sri Chinmoy explains the secrets of death, the afterlife and reincarnation. $7.95

Yoga and the Spiritual Life
Specifically tailored for Western readers, this book offers rare insight into the philosophy of Yoga and Eastern mysticism. $8.95

The Summits of God-Life:
Samadhi and Siddhi
A genuine account of the world beyond time and space, this is Sri Chinmoy's first-hand account of states of consciousness that only a handful of Masters have ever experienced. $6.95

The Three Branches of India's Life-Tree:
Commentaries on the Vedas,
the Upanishads and the Bhagavad Gita

This book is both an excellent introduction for readers who are coming to these Hindu classics for the first time, and a series of illumining meditations for those who already know them well. $13.95

Kundalini: The Mother-Power

Sri Chinmoy explains techniques for awakening the Kundalini and the chakras, warns of the dangers and pitfalls to be avoided, and discusses some of the occult powers that can be developed. $7.95

The Inner Promise:
Sri Chinmoy's University Talks

Speaking in a state of deep meditation during these 42 talks, Sri Chinmoy filled the audience with a serenity many had never before experienced. They found his words, as a faculty member later put it, to be "living seeds of spirituality." $14.95

Everest-Aspiration

Inspired talks on a wide variety of spiritual themes.
$9.95

A Child's Heart and a Child's Dream: Growing Up with Spiritual Wisdom—
A Guide for Parents and Children

Sri Chinmoy offers practical advice on fostering your child's spiritual life, watching him or her grow up with a love of God and a heart of self-giving. $7.95

The Master and the Disciple

Sri Chinmoy says in this definitive book on the Guru-disciple relationship: "The most important thing a Guru does for his spiritual children is to make them aware of something vast and infinite within themselves, which is nothing other than God Himself." $7.95

Siddhartha Becomes the Buddha

The combination of profound insight and simplicity of language makes this book an excellent choice for anyone, young or old, seeking to understand one of the world's most influential spiritual figures. $6.95

Music by Sri Chinmoy

Flute Music for Meditation
While in a state of deep meditation, Sri Chinmoy plays his haunting melodies on the echo flute. Ideal for inspiration in your personal meditation.

Cassette, $9.95   CD, $12.95

The Dance of Light:
Sri Chinmoy Plays the Flute
Forty-seven soft and gentle flute melodies that will carry you directly to the source of joy and beauty: your own aspiring heart.   Cassette, $9.95

Ecstasy's Trance:
Esraj Music for Meditation
The esraj, often described as a soothing combination of sitar and violin, is Sri Chinmoy's favourite instrument. With haunting intensity, he seems to draw the music from another dimension.

Cassette, $9.95